First World War
and Army of Occupation
War Diary
France, Belgium and Germany

31 DIVISION
94 Infantry Brigade
Royal Welsh Fusiliers
24th Battalion
2 May 1918 - 30 April 1919

WO95/2366/4

The Naval & Military Press Ltd
www.nmarchive.com
Published in association with The National Archives

Published by

The Naval & Military Press Ltd

Unit 10 Ridgewood Industrial Park,
Uckfield, East Sussex,
TN22 5QE England
Tel: +44 (0) 1825 749494

www.naval-military-press.com

www.nmarchive.com

This diary has been reprinted in facsimile from the original. Any imperfections are inevitably reproduced and the quality may fall short of modern type and cartographic standards.

© Crown Copyright
Images reproduced by permission of The National Archives, London, England, 2015.

Contents

Document type	Place/Title	Date From	Date To
Heading	WO95/2366-4 24 Battalion Royal Welsh Fusiliers		
Heading	31st Division 94th Infy Bde 24th Bn Roy. Welsh Fus. (Denbigh Yeomanry Bn) May 1918-Apr 1919 From Egypt 74 Dn 231 Bde		
Heading	74th Division 231st Infy Bde 31 Div 94 Bde 24th Bn Roy. Welsh Fus. May-1918		
War Diary	At Sea	02/05/1918	06/05/1918
War Diary	Marseilles	07/05/1918	08/05/1918
War Diary	Train	09/05/1918	11/05/1918
War Diary	Domvast	12/05/1918	22/05/1918
War Diary	Moncheaux	23/05/1918	24/05/1918
War Diary	Hauteville	25/05/1918	31/05/1918
Heading	War Diary Of The 24th Denbigh Yeomanry Battalion Royal Welsh Fusiliers. Volume June 1918 XXVIII Period: From June 1st, 1918. To June 30th, 1918		
War Diary	Hauteville (J 35)	01/06/1918	20/06/1918
War Diary	Lynde Area	21/06/1918	24/06/1918
War Diary	D. 18.a.	25/06/1918	30/06/1918
Heading	War Diary. 24th (Denbigh Hussars Yeomanry) Battalion Royal Welsh Fusiliers. Volume 2 1918 Period: From July 1st, 1918, To July 31st, 1918 Vol 4		
War Diary	E. 27.d. 7.9.	01/07/1918	05/07/1918
War Diary	E. 10.d. 11.	06/07/1918	07/07/1918
War Diary	E 25d. 26	08/07/1918	09/07/1918
War Diary	D. 9.a. 3.7	10/07/1918	15/07/1918
War Diary	E. 7b 80.55.	16/07/1918	19/07/1918
War Diary	E. 7b 80.85.	20/07/1918	24/07/1918
War Diary	D 6d 98.	20/07/1918	31/07/1918
Heading	War Diary 24th (Denbigh Yeomanry) Bn. Royal Welsh Fusiliers. Vol III Period:- August 1st 1918 To August 31st 1918		
War Diary		01/08/1918	31/08/1918
Heading	War Diary 24th (Denbigh Yeo) Battalion Royal Welsh Fusiliers. Vol. IV Period:- Sept 1st 1918 To Sept 30th 1918		
War Diary	Fletre	01/09/1918	03/09/1918
War Diary	Bailleul	04/09/1918	04/09/1918
War Diary	Hill 63 (T.18.C)	05/09/1918	12/09/1918
War Diary	S. 9d.	13/09/1918	15/09/1918
War Diary	S 21c	16/09/1918	17/09/1918
War Diary	T 28a	18/09/1918	19/09/1918
War Diary	T 23d. Petit Monque Farm	20/09/1918	21/09/1918
War Diary	T 23d.	21/09/1918	24/09/1918
War Diary	Hondeghem	25/09/1918	27/09/1918
War Diary	T 25 C 1.1. (Sheet 28)	28/09/1918	28/09/1918
War Diary	U. 14a Central	29/09/1918	30/09/1918
Heading	War Diary 24th (Denbigh Yeo.) Bn. R. Welsh Fusiliers October 1918 Volume V Period:- October 1st 1918 To October 31st 1918		
War Diary	X 24a 3.4.	01/10/1918	05/10/1918

War Diary	T 18. C 31	06/10/1918	08/10/1918
War Diary	U 16b. 8.5.	09/10/1918	12/10/1918
War Diary	U. 16b 8.3	13/10/1918	15/10/1918
War Diary	T 25 C 1.4	16/10/1918	16/10/1918
War Diary	U 23 b. 1.7	17/10/1918	19/10/1918
War Diary	G 16a. 75 99	20/10/1918	24/10/1918
War Diary	G. 16 a. 77.90 S. 22 a 99	25/10/1918	25/10/1918
War Diary	S 22 a 99	26/10/1918	26/10/1918
War Diary	I 20 Central	27/10/1918	28/10/1918
War Diary	P 7 b 2.8	29/10/1918	30/10/1918
War Diary	P 7 C. 2.8	31/10/1918	31/10/1918
Heading	War Diary 24th. (Denbigh Yeo.) Bn. Royal Welsh Fusiliers. November 1918 Vol VI Period:- Nov. 1st 1918 To Nov. 30th. 1918		
War Diary	P 6. C.2.8.	01/11/1918	02/11/1918
War Diary	Sheet 29 M. 14c. 8.3.	03/11/1918	09/11/1918
War Diary	P 27 a. 6.2.	10/11/1918	10/11/1918
War Diary	X 16 C 55	11/11/1918	12/11/1918
War Diary	X 18 C 98	13/11/1918	13/11/1918
War Diary	Sheet 29 Dic 75	14/10/1918	14/10/1918
War Diary	M 14 C. 8.3.	15/10/1918	24/10/1918
War Diary	Sheet 28 Q S B 4.2.	25/10/1918	25/10/1918
War Diary	1/Hazebrouck ZI	26/11/1918	26/11/1918
War Diary	3G	27/11/1918	27/11/1918
War Diary	4 E	28/11/1918	28/11/1918
War Diary	4 C	29/11/1918	30/11/1918
Heading	War Diary 24th (Denbigh Yeo) Bn. Royal Welsh Fusiliers December 1918 Volume VII Period:- December 1st 1918 to December 31st 1918.		
War Diary	St Omer Combined Sheet X 7 Central	01/12/1918	11/12/1918
War Diary	Sheet 36 O East 5d.	12/12/1918	12/12/1918
War Diary	St. Omer Combined-Sheet	17/12/1918	18/12/1918
War Diary	W 25 C.4.8.	19/12/1918	24/12/1918
War Diary	St. Omer Combined Sheet	25/12/1918	26/12/1918
War Diary	W. 25 C. 48	27/12/1918	31/12/1918
Heading	War Diary 24th. (Denbigh Yeo) Bn. Royal Welsh Fusiliers. Jan. 1919 Vol VIII Period. Jan 1st. 1919 To Jan 31st. 1919		
War Diary	St Omer Combined Sheet W 25 C. 4.8.	01/01/1919	31/01/1919
Heading	War Diary 24th (Denbigh Yeo) Bn. R. Welsh Fusiliers February 1919 Volume 38 Period February 1st 1919 To February 28th 1919		
War Diary	Hondeghem Staging Camp	01/02/1919	18/02/1919
War Diary	Hondighem	19/02/1919	28/02/1919
Heading	War Diary 24th (Denbigh Yeo) Bn R. Welsh Fusiliers. March 1919 Volume XXXIX Period:- March 1st 1919 To March 31st 1919		
War Diary	Hondighem	01/03/1919	04/03/1919
War Diary	St. Omer	05/03/1919	30/04/1919

WO/95/2369/4

24 Battalion Royal Welsh Fusiliers

31ST DIVISION
94TH INFY BDE

24TH BN ROY. WELSH FUS.
(DENBIGH YEOMANRY BN)
MAY 1918 – APR 1919

FROM EGYPT 74 DN 231 BDE

ATTACHED { 74TH DIVISION
231ST INFY BDE

31 DIV
94 BDE

24TH BN ROY. WELSH FUS.
MAY- 1918

# WAR DIARY / INTELLIGENCE SUMMARY

2nd (Denbighshire) Bn. R.W.F.

Army Form C. 2118.
VOLUME XXVI
Sheet 1

Ref map ABBEVILLE 1:100000

S. Marshall

May 16

Hour, Date, Place			Summary of Events and Information	Remarks and references to Appendices
1700	May 2nd	at Sea	Nil	2/Lt
1800	" 3rd	"	"	2/Lt
1200	" 4	"	"	2/Lt
1500	" 5	"	"	2/Lt
1700	" 6	"	"	2/Lt
1900	" 7	MARSEILLES	Disembarked at MARSEILLES – and marched to Camp Moussot 36 officers 775 O.Rs. Strong.	2/Lt
2100	" 8	"	Nil	2/Lt
2000	" 9	TRAIN	Entrained at MARSEILLES 21530	2/Lt
1200	" 10	"	Nil	2/Lt
1700	" 11	"	Nil	2/Lt
0900	" 12	DOMVAST	Arrived NOYELLES 1000 – Bttn marched to DOMVAST and went into billets.	2/Lt
1700	" 13	"	Rain all day – cleaning up – 5 O.R. to hospital	2/Lt
1200	" 13	"	COs Kit inspection. Company training. 4 O.R. to hospital	2/Lt
1100	" 14	"	333 O.Rs marched to NOUVION to Divisional Baths.	2/Lt
0500	" 15	"	Lecture by Lt Colonel CAMPBELL on Bayonet Fighting.	2/Lt
			4 H.D. Horses 1 Rd mule 1 Mallens and 1 Machine Gun drawn from ABBEVILLE. 3 O.R. to Hospital	2/Lt
1500	" 16	"	353 O.Rs to NOUVION to bathe – chemical Advisor VII Corps gave lectures 9 am to 12 noon and 2 pm to 3 pm.	2/Lt
1400	" 17	"	1 O.R. to Hospital.	2/Lt
1100	" 18	"	Nil	2/Lt

Army Form C. 2118

WAR DIARY
or
INTELLIGENCE SUMMARY

Instructions regarding War Diaries and Intelligence 24th (Durham) Bn D.L.I.
Summaries are contained in F.S. Regs., Part II.
and the Staff Manual respectively. Title Pages
will be prepared in manuscript.

(Erase heading not required.) Ref Map ABBEVILLE 1/100000

VOLUME XXVI
Sheet 2
LENS 1/100000

Place	Date	Hour	Summary of Events and Information	Remarks and references to Appendices
DOMVAST	May 19	10 am	Nil	A/H
"	20	3 pm	Battalion route march — 5 O.R. to Hospital. Capts A.T. Maughan rejoined from leave in U.K. Extract from London Gazette 10/5/1/8 2/Lt (acting Capt & Adj) R.I. HODGES to be Capt. and remain as Adjt 31/18/17 Lt A.R. COONEY to be Capt 14/2/18	A/H
"	21	8 am	3 O.R. to Hospital. Company training.	A/H
"	22	4 pm	Battalion left DOMVAST to entrain at RUE	
MONCHEAUX	23	6 pm	Battalion entrained at RUE – Hqrs and C Company at 5:24 am. A B & D Companies at 9:34 am. Detrained at LIGNY ST FLOCHEL and marched into billets at MONCHEAUX.	A/H
"	24	11 am	Very wet — received orders to move on 25th inst to HAUTEVILLE.	A/H
HAUTEVILLE	25	5 pm	Battalion marched into billets at HAUTEVILLE via following routes, opened to details into two battalions. LA PERTE, L.A. BLOCKLEY, 2Lt ETP THOMAS, 2Lt CH MILLER, 2Lt FW SAVOURS.	A/H
"	26	10 am	Rifle and Musketry. 1 Company musketry on 30 range. 57 O.R. reinforcements arrived.	A/H
"	27	8 am	Rifle and Musketry on range — 13 O.R. Reinforcements arrived Captains and staff officers & 2 company commanders lecture for tour in trenches	A/H
"	28	10 am	Company training — 2 company commanders leave for tour in trenches	A/H
"	29	3 pm	G.O.C. 24 Division inspected battalion on parade. 4 O.R. to hospital.	A/H
"	30	3 pm	Battalion firing on target range. Company officers and 3 Company Commanders attended Traffic Control Lecture from Provost Marshall Lt CP KNIGHTLEY Mounted 24th Division	A/H

WAR DIARY
INTELLIGENCE SUMMARY

Army Form C. 2118

Instructions regarding War Diaries and Intelligence are contained in F.S. Regs., Part II. Summaries are contained in F. S. Regs., Part II. and the Staff Manual respectively. Title Pages will be prepared in manuscript.

2nd (Donbighshire) RWF
Volume XXVII
Sheet 8

Map. LENS 1:10,000

(Erase heading not required.)

Place	Date	Hour	Summary of Events and Information	Remarks and references to Appendices
HAUTEVILLE	May 1	8 am	Nil	A/6

John Russ.
Lt Colonel
Cmd. 2/1st (Denbigh yo) RWRF.

CONFIDENTIAL.

WAR DIARY

OF

THE 24TH (DENBIGH YEOMANRY BATTALION) ROYAL WELSH FUSILIERS.

VOLUME

JUNE, 1918.

XXVIII.

Apr 1919.

PERIOD : From June 1st, 1918.
To June 30th, 1918.

CONFIDENTIAL.

24th (Denbigh Yeo) Bn R.W.F.

Army Form C. 2118.

WAR DIARY
or
INTELLIGENCE SUMMARY.

(Erase heading not required.)

Volume XXVIII Reel 1. June 1918. Ref Map 5/c 1/40,000

Place	Date	Hour	Summary of Events and Information	Remarks and references to Appendices
HAUTEVILLE (J55)	1918. June 1	7 pm	Brigade Field Day in neighbourhood of BEAUFORT. Capt R.J. Hodges to Major 2318 Bn. for duty. Lieut B.E. Benton appointed Actg. Adjutant. 12 OR to L.Leave, U.K. 4 officers + 120 R to Brigade Rural Course	
"	2nd	5 pm	Divine Service - Capt A.B. Cooney appointed 2 in Command of C. Coy, transferred from HQrs. Lt. E.R. Niello from HQrs to HQrs as Acty. Asst Adjutant. LR. Franklin from D. Coy to HQrs as L.E. officer	
"	3rd	8.30 pm	Battalion Field Operations near HAUTEVILLE - Lecture to all officers by Brig. Gen. Heathcote at LATTRE ST QUENTIN - 2 OR to hospital	
"	4th	7 pm	Battalion marched to LATTRE ST QUENTIN for Lectures & demonstrations by Divisional Gas Officer - 2 OR to hospital	
"	5th	6 pm	Brigade Field day in MONTENESCOURT AREA - 2 OR to Infantry Base ROUEN	
"	6th	5 pm	Battalion Field Operations near WAN QUENTIN. 2 Coys bathing at FOSSEUX	
"	7th	8 pm	Battalion training near HAUTEVILLE. Major H.J. HOWELL-EVANS, Capt C.L. FOSSERY and Capt R.C. LLOYD left for rest at the Trenches. 2 Coys + HQrs to bathe FOSSEUX	
"	8th	7.30 pm	Brigade Field Day in neighbourhood of BEAUFORT. 1 OR to Infantry Base ROUEN	
"	9th	8 pm	Divine Service. Received news to be ready to move at 9 hours notice. Party returned from L.Leave Down	
"	10th	6 pm	Battalion in Field in cooperation with 6 "Sports". 20 paraphots remain Capt A.B. Cooney to Musketry Course HAZEBROUCK. 30 OR reinforcements	
"	11th	9 pm	Battalion training at HAUTEVILLE - Capt J.B. SPRINGMAN to U.K. 3 mos. leave	
"	12th	7 pm	Company training. 2/Lt R.W. SERLE (Pamphlets/Gas) reported. Capt C.L. FOSBERY from 10 OR to L.Leave, U.K.	
"	13th		Lewis Gun training - Battalion throw serves Aves to throw instruments	

Army Form C. 2118.

WAR DIARY
or
INTELLIGENCE SUMMARY

24th (Barbados) Bn Royal Welsh Fusiliers

Ref Maps 51c 1/40,000
36a. N.W. 1/20,000

Volume XXVIII Sheet 2

(Erase heading not required.)

Place	Date	Hour	Summary of Events and Information	Remarks and references to Appendices
HAUTEVILLE 35.	1918 June 14th	4.30pm	Lewis Gun Training for whole Battalion	AWS
"	15th	8am	Lewis Gun Training	AWS
"	16th	5pm	Voluntary Divine Service. Hon. Capt. & Qm T. Brand to Laton Corps Base Depot, BOULOGNE.	AWS
"	17th	6.30pm	Company Training. Published in General Orders. E.H.H. ALLENBY's despatch (Anglesea) in London Gazette 14/6/18. Hon Capt & Qm T. BRAND (Butlinghurst) 30 out 24 R.W.F. 345170 A.S.M. CRINYION. 2nd W.W.F.	AWS
"	18th	8am	Company & Specialist Training. 2nd Lt E J PHILLIPS - 2nd W J MARSTON c/o-OR to Arm U.K. 340 H.Q. HOWELL EVANS to 10 KSLI (to command Battn) Capt R C LLOYD to are to command	AWS
"	19th	8am	nil	AWS
"	20th 21st	9.30am	Farm leave U.K. 1.O.R. - made by farewell by GENERALS BIRDWOOD & HEATHCOTE Bn having been transferred to 31st Div minus to 2nd Army Area, entraining at TINQUES, & detraining at BLARINGHAM. Billeted in LYNDE area. 24th R.W.F., 12th R.W.F., & 12th Norfolks on pairs new 93 Brigade, taking place of 4th Guards Brigade."	L.2.R.R
LYNDE AREA	22nd 23rd		Divine Service. Fitting of P.B.R. - TO F.2 Ant. 2nd Lt F.W.R. HOUGH 11 O.R. Capt. DIVE RAPS nil. Struck off strength 21st	5-9-43

A.102560 Wt 5300/P713 750,000 2/18 Sch. 53 'Forms/C2118/16
D. D. & L., London, E.C.

Army Form C. 2118.

WAR DIARY
or
INTELLIGENCE SUMMARY.

2/4th A Denbigh Yeo. Bn. Royal Welsh Fusiliers

Ref. In ops. 36ª N.W. 1/20000
36ª N.E. 1/20000

Instructions regarding War Diaries and Intelligence Summaries are contained in F.S. Regs. Part II. and the Staff Manual respectively. Title pages will be prepared in manuscript. Volume XXVIII Sheet 3

(Erase heading not required.)

Place	Date	Hour	Summary of Events and Information	Remarks and references to Appendices
LYNDE AREA	24th	1.30pm	Bn. moved to MORBECQUE.	
	25th	6.30pm	Bn. moved into Brigade Reserve, into the "B" line. Little activity - 1 O.R. slightly wounded.	W.R.
D.18.a.			Lt. LEWIS, Lt.COLE & 2/Lt HEARNS to leave U.K. from leave U.K. 3 O.Rs. 32 O.Rs rejoined. "A" Coy supplied working & covering party at night.	W.R. W.R.
D.18.a.	26th	6.30pm	Little activity - Gas shells in area at 9.00 pm for 1 hour	W.R.
"	24th	7.30pm	3 Coys. Bn. Digging night 26-27th. Houby night - rain in progress - little activity all day -	W.R.
"	28th	4.30pm	Bn. acted as carrying party for 92nd Brigade, when latter captured enemy position GARST BRUGGHE, GOMBERT FARM and VERTETRUE - Battalion disposed as follows - No.1 Party - CAPT. A.J. MAYHEW & 2 officers and 190 O.Rs. of B Coy & 10 officers 3.0 O.Rs. of B Coy acting under orders of O.C. 211 Coy R.E. No.2 Party - 2nd LT. SEXLE 60 OR of D.Coy attached to 10th EAST YORKS. REGT. under orders of O.C. 10th E.Y.R. This party met tail of 10th E.Y.R. at 11.00 pm 27th at E.27.d.40. on "A" RIDE. No.3 Party - (a) 2nd LT. SAVOURS & 60 OR. as follows - 30 OR A Coy, 20 OR C Coy, 10 OR B Coy - met tail of 11th E.Y.R. junction of A Ride & No.3. track (tramway) at 11 pm. (b) LT. A.T. THOMAS & 90 O.R. left for K & L dumps at same time as (a). No.4 Party - 2nd LT. E.T.P. THOMAS & 60 OR. of B Coy met tail of 11th E. LANCS REGT at SPOOR COTTAGE at 10 pm. & moved forward with them.	W.R.

WAR DIARY or INTELLIGENCE SUMMARY

Army Form C. 2118.

24th (Denbigh Yeo) Bn. Royal Welch Fusiliers

Ref. Maps. 36 A NE. 1/20,000

Volume XVII Sheet 4

Place	Date	Hour	Summary of Events and Information	Remarks and references to Appendices
D.18.a.	28th	7.30p.m.	No. 5. Party – Lt KNIGHT & 60 O.R. of D.Coy. met tail of 10th L.Y.R. at 11.½p.m. All parties were employed carrying material for consolidating posts – A.B.C.D.E.F.G.H. Enemy position was captured by 7.30 A.M. with heavy loss to the enemy – Bn. parties returned at various times during the day – Total casualties killed 2 O.R. Missing 2 O.R. wounded 2ND LT. E.T.R.THOMAS & 52 O.R.	W.S.R.
"	29th	7.30pm	Night 28-29th Whole Battalion out working – 2ND LT SAVOURS & 50 O.R. arrived afternoon of 28th from "B" Team & proceeded to Camp to the front line – was caught in between our own & the enemy's barrage – 1 O.R. wounded – Remainder of parties had no casualties –	W.S.R.
"	30th	7.30pm	Bn. took over front line from 4 Battalions with R.S.F. on right & flank – Bn. moved off past TETTLE FARM at 10.00, & completed relief by 2.00 am. Enemy shelled front line heavily during relief – Casualties 1 O.R. wounded (Capt Wolley) Position, E. of FOREST DE NIEPPE.	W.S.R.
E.29.d.4.4.				

J. W. ?
Captain
O.C. 24th Bn. R. Welch Fus.

CONFIDENTIAL.

WAR DIARY.

24TH (DENBIGH HUSSARS YEOMANRY) BATTALION ROYAL WELSH FUSILIERS.

VOLUME 2

1918.

PERIOD : From July 1st, 1918,
To July 31st, 1918.

Army Form C. 2118.

WAR DIARY
or
INTELLIGENCE SUMMARY.
(Erase heading not required.)

1/4 (Anbgh Yos) Bn. R.W.F.

Instructions regarding War Diaries and Intelligence Summaries are contained in F.S. Regs., Part II. and the Staff Manual respectively. Title pages will be prepared in manuscript. VOLUME XXIX Sheet 1

Ref. Map – 36a. N.E. 1/20,000.

Place	Date	Hour	Summary of Events and Information	Remarks and references to Appendices
E.27.d.7.9.	1st July	7.30a	Bn. holding front line, three from N. to S. – C.A.B. Coys. D. in Support, two Platoons at BEAULIEU FARM, & two platoons with Bn. H.Q. Artillery walker active.	6.7.R.B.
	2nd	10pm	1 O.R. Killed at Bn. HQ. with shrapnel – Bn. in front line – Artillery again active – New Bn. Defence Scheme came into force night 2nd/3rd. 2 Coys in front line, 2 Coys in Support – E28, and E22 and	6.7.R.B.
	3rd	11pm	Supervision given in accordance with new Scheme. Artillery active. Reconnaissance at VIEUX BERQUIN. Artillery quiet. Light patrols reconnoitred PLATE BECQUE 11am to 2am. Nothing further – 1 O.R in Hospital	6.7.S
	4th	10pm	Both artilleries quiet all day. 9pm enemy barrage on days brigade. Patrols again reconnoitred PLATE BECQUE and brought in one enemy M.G. from E.30.a.06. Enemy artillery moderately active. 2 OR wounded.	6.7.S
	5th	11.30p	Lieut J.F. Rotogen (I.D.) to gutting. Our artillery kept up harassing fire, enemy artillery quiet. Patrol 1 NCO + 3 men reconnoitred track over BECQUE at E.30.a.44. R.E. blew up tree roads at E.29.d.06. + E.29.d.59.	6.7.S
E.10.d.11.	6th	10.30pm	Artillery quiet. Battalion relieved by 12. R.S.F. moved into Brigade Reserve. HQ at E.10.d.11. D Coy. E.20.a.91. A Coy. E.27.a.25. B Coy. E.27.a.25. C Coy E.25.a.33.	6.7.S
	7th	8pm	Hostile artillery searched wood with 4.2s + 5.9s	6.7.S
E.25.a.56.	8th	9pm	HQ moved from E.10.d.11 to E.25.a.2.6. Hostile artillery active searching wood. 1 OR wounded.	6.7.S
	9th	11pm	Both artilleries active, especially at night	6.7.S

WAR DIARY or INTELLIGENCE SUMMARY

Army Form C. 2118.

24 (Pontypridd) Bn R. Welsh Fus.

VOL. XXIX Sheet 2.

Ref Map Sheet 36ᴬ N.E. 1/20,000

Place	Date	Hour	Summary of Events and Information	Remarks and references to Appendices
D.9.a.3.7.	July 10ᵗʰ	10 pm	Batt alien relieved by 15 Bn. W. Yorks Regt. (92 Bde) and moved back into Divisional Reserve at D.9.a.3.9. 4 companies in D.9.a. - D.9.c.	A.W.d.
	11ᵗʰ	8 pm	Baths	B.W.l.
	12ᵗʰ	9.30 am	S.R.d.	C.W.S.
	13ᵗʰ	9 pm	B.O.R. Inspection by G.O.C. 94 Bde.	D.W.S.
	14ᵗʰ	8.15 pm	Inspection by G.O.C. 15ᵗʰ Corps.	E.W.S.
	15ᵗʰ	10 pm	Gas Projector demonstration	
	16ᵗʰ	11 pm	Battn relieved 10ᵗʰ East Yorks. Taking up a position numbered N.T.S. being left Battn of the Brigade. D. and B. Coys being in front line E.11.b and E.11.a. A. Coy in support. C. Coy W.E.15.a.b as Reserve. E.17.a, E.17.d. I.O.R. Killed in front line by a sniper.	F.W.S.
E.7.b 80.55	17ᵗʰ	10 pm	Enemy artillery active all day. Our artillery retaliated. Enemy Trench Mortar Reamt for 24 hours.	G.W.S.
	18ᵗʰ	8.15 pm	The whole of 17/18 B. Coy Patrol of 1 Off. (2/Lt England) and 23 O.Rs. Proceeded to E.17.d.4.5 to attack enemy M.G. encountered no enemy. An enemy M.G. located at house E.17.d.6.9. Enemy artillery fairly active during the night. 2/Lt Earle with 21 O.Rs. E.11.b.4.0 N. to E.17.b.80.95. To occupied part H. and during patrolling found suspected position near E.17.b.69 and from information of Prisoner later M.G.'s operating in this locality patrolling was unsuccessful owning to enemy flare	
			Casualties - 1 Officer 30 O.Rs wounded 10 O.R. missing	
	19ᵗʰ	9 pm	Enemy artillery heavy and active shelling our front line & support. The whole night 18/19ᵗʰ 8.20 pm 2/Lt T. Williams and 21 O.Rs. Proceeded to locate enemy Post at E.17.d.4.5 but found area occupied by enemy outside M.G. fire. 2/Lt Brown (attd) & Sergeant seriously wounded.	H.W.S.

Army Form C. 2118.

WAR DIARY
or
INTELLIGENCE SUMMARY.

(Erase heading not required.)

1/1 (Pembeigh. Yeo) Bn. R.Welsh. Fus.

Instructions regarding War Diaries and Intelligence
Summaries are contained in F.S. Regs., Part II.
and the Staff Manual respectively. Title pages
will be prepared in manuscript. VOL XXX Sheet 2

REF MAP. SHEET 36A N.E. 1/20,000

Place	Date	Hour	Summary of Events and Information	Remarks and references to Appendices
E.17.b.80.85.	20th	10pm	2/Lt Mennie and 2 O.R's left our lines on the night of 19-20th at 11.15 pm to locate enemy posts reported E.17.b.50. but had to withdraw at 1 a.m. owing to eg. 1. O.R. slightly gassed. Enemy artillery was fairly active. Casualties: 1. O.R. wounded.	See.
	21st	9.30pm	1 Officer and 3 O.R's left our lines to locate enemy posts. After patrolling 400 yards, they were fired on by enemy flanks and E.12.c.65.25. and 10th were wounded. According to orders at 7.45pm At 4.80 pm 2/Lt England and 3 O.R's left Authie Farm, to locate enemy posts. Patrol found enemy posts at E.17.a.98. The same patrol left again at 10.30 pm and located enemy M.G. emplacements E.17.b.66. which were unoccupied. Enemy patrol was heard moving to our lines. Casualties:- 3. O.R's wounded.	See.
	22nd	10.15 pm	On the night of 21-22nd the Batt. boundary with the 12th Norfolks took over the point occupied by our right platoon. Our new front Batt. boundary our left being E.17.b.74. to E.15.b.20. 1 Officer & 7 O.R's left our lines E.11.b.52 to locate enemy positions east of that point. Enemy M.G. fire was opened on our parties on lines E.17.b.76. E.17.b.86. E.17.b.36. Patrol returned 6.20 pm At 6.30pm 1 Officer & 5 O.R's left our lines E.11.b.52 to reconnoitre position & enemy establishment. Starting Point. The Patrol proceeded 400 yds	See.

Army Form C. 2118.

WAR DIARY
or
INTELLIGENCE SUMMARY.

24 (Denbigh Yeo) Bn. R.Welsh.Fus.

Instructions regarding War Diaries and Intelligence Summaries are contained in F.S. Regs., Part II. and the Staff Manual respectively. Title pages will be prepared in manuscript. Vol XXX Sheet 4.

REF MAP. SHEET 36A N.E. 1:20,000.

Place	Date	Hour	Summary of Events and Information	Remarks and references to Appendices
E76 80 85.				
	23	10.15pm	The 6" Newtons and Stokes and M.G. fire from friendly batteries fired in battery directions but east to withdraw owing to heavy M.G. fire from enemy held Post E12c62 and from Cold Knuckle Trench from E12c23. E18a67. Enemy shelled our support line heavily, 2h.15-3.45pm area Viciose Rosaburry causing fires. 1 O.R. killed (remained at duty). Casualties. 1 O.R. wounded. 1 O.R. wounded.	S.S.S. Officer wounded
	24	11pm	The enclosure E17b46-E17b86 to E17b76-E17b4870 NE of Fm was raided by 2/8 Sherwoods and 300 O.Rs. Our artillery heavily shelled the area preparatory to raid. The closure was found to be unoccupied. This may be due to the fact that the enemy posts were being relieved. Enemy artillery retaliated on our support lines during the raid. 2/8 Sherwoods and 10 O.Rs preceded the attacking Post E112 80 was occupied. The patrol met with no opposition and reached objective. Seeing no signs of enemy withdrew. 2/8 Sherwoods and 10 O.Rs left our lines at 1am to reconnoitre enemy posts at E117 & 55.80. Encountered enemy about 12 of 10's enemy patrol had advanced up 50yds from his lines, our patrol rushed them & M.G. and Lewis guns opened fire. Enemy fled leaving behind a Lewis gun and falling back towards falling place of Jerusalem Trench.	

Army Form C. 2118.

WAR DIARY
or
INTELLIGENCE SUMMARY

(Erase heading not required.)

24th Denbigh Yeo. Bn. R. Welsh Fus.

Instructions regarding War Diaries and Intelligence Summaries are contained in F.S. Regs., Part II. and the Staff Manual respectively. Title pages will be prepared in manuscript. Vol XXX Sheet 5.

REF. MAP. SHEET 36a. N.E. 1:20000

Place	Date	Hour	Summary of Events and Information	Remarks and references to Appendices
E.7b.8.0.'85"	25.		cited. The enemy M.G. opened fire, burst of several bullets off the porch to right of entry of drive to our trenches. Eventually after this movement being observed, had to withdraw. Casualties. 3.O.R. wounded, one of whom missing.	P.S.S.
D.6.d.9.8.		11.30p	The Battn. was relieved by the 12 R.S.F. and moved to Reserve reserve at D.6.d.9.8. (C.A. Coys at Grandcourt, Fm. B. Coy at A.P.a. Promenade. D. Coy Grand. See B.O.S. During day enemy Artillery and aircraft quiet.	
	26.	10pm – 1.30am	Reprisal shoot by Batteries of Reserve. Working party sent out, and not interfered with. Enemy Artillery and aircraft quiet.	P.S.S.
	27.	9.30pm	Our Artillery active during the hours of 3–5.30 pm. Working party sent to R.E.'s.	P.S.S.
	28.	11.30pm	Relieved by 18 Bn Durham Light Infantry (93 Bde) and our Battn. moved back into Divisional Reserve at D.9.a to 57. Companies in D.9. D.9.b.c. E.9347 was bombed earlier in the evening our advance party suffered 4 Casualties. 1 Officer 3 O.R.s. 1 O.R. wounded on duty.	P.S.S.
	29.	10 pm	Baths, and Cleaning up.	P.S.S.
	30.	9.30pm	Companies inspected by C.O.	P.S.S.
	31.	10pm	The night of the 30 to 31st the Battn. had orders to stand to. Firing on rifle range of 30 yds. in course of the day. Acting Major on 2nd R. W.F.	P.S.S.

CONFIDENTIAL.

WAR DIARY.

24ᵀᴴ (DENBIGH YEOMANRY) BN. ROYAL WELSH FUSILIERS.

VOL. III.

PERIOD :— AUGUST 1ˢᵀ 1918
           To
           AUGUST 31ˢᵀ 1918.

Army Form C. 2118.

WAR DIARY
or
INTELLIGENCE SUMMARY.

24th (DEN. YEO) BAT. R.W.F.

REF. SHEET. 26.

Instructions regarding War Diaries and Intelligence Summaries are contained in F.S. Regs., Part II. and the Staff Manual respectively. Title pages will be prepared in manuscript. Vol XXXII Sheet 1.

(Erase heading not required.)

Place	Date	Hour	Summary of Events and Information	Remarks and references to Appendices
	August 1917			
	1.	1.40 pm	Company arrangements.	See A.9
	2.	9.15.	Company parade. Cooperation with aircraft.	See A.9
	3.	11 pm	Company parade. Lieut Colonel H.N.M.CLEGG returned from leave taking over command of the Battalion. The Battalion relieved the 15 WEST YORKS REGT. A & B. Companies going into the front line, left & right respectively and C and D Coys into "Z" Line. BAT.H.Q. E.17 d 85.60.	See A.9
	4.	11.15 pm	Relief complete at 1.20 a.m. FM Patrolling finding no enemy in strength. 1 N.C.O. 3 O.Rs. to reconnoitre the W360 NE. of TERN FM and finding no enemy returned.	See A.9
	5.	11.55pm	2/Lt D.R.MILES proceeded with I O.R. to E.17 a.51. no enemy to be seen. at E.17 d. 5.6 he observed a belt of wire but did not venture to there relieved to E.17 d.4.4. place of exit. Corporals 2. DAVIES, G. KIRBY. 2/Lt D.R.MILES and 2.O.R. proceeded to E.17 d. 5.6 intended to and Reconnaissance disclosed This to be occupied. as he while to there two suspected the post continuing the M.G. and enemy numbered of 5 gunners. 2/Lt D.R.MAES. again went out and attacked an Enemy M.G.post at E.18 a 4.8. which he and Cpl. 3.O.Rs rushed capturing the M.G. 10 shell of 5 R. killed 2 sent back under escort of 2.O.Rs. were their Proceeded with his I.O.R. to E.18 a 4.8. a distance of 280 yds where they encountered a	See A.9

WAR DIARY or INTELLIGENCE SUMMARY

24(DEN:YED) BAT. R.W.F.

REF. SHEET 28.

Army Form C. 2118.

Vol XXXII Sheet 2

Place	Date	Hour	Summary of Events and Information	Remarks and references to Appendices
	6/7		M.G. post referred to in last entry was rushed and found to be held by 4 men the rest of the enemy being taken prisoners.	988.
			2/ Pt. FERGUSON of 2.O.R. proceeded at 2.45 p.m. to E.18.a.38 where he observed several patrols who appeared to have been unoccupied for some time gaining this information he returned.	
		11.25 pm	2/Lt. J.W. Edwards and 2.O.R. proceeded to M.G. post at 6.15 p.m. where he found the M.G. Crew relieved and ammunition by the Crew.	988.
	7/7		2/Lt. D.R. MILES proceeded with patrol to E.M.D.57 and onwards to E.M.D.57 and onwards on L.G. post finding one M.G. post unoccupied. Sent M.G. post onwards on L.G. post finding very good information.	
		11.30 pm	2/Lt. D.R. MILES again went out at 10 pm pushing 2 M.Q posts which the enemy began reconnoitring occasion. he also noticed other patrols which were out after dark. "A" Company advanced their line 250 yds. so straightening out the left Brigade from the trenches.	988.
	7/8		2/Lt. D.R. MILES with 2.O.R. proceeded to E.N.E.9.5 from which he observed enemy occupying glass huts who were firing a Machine gun and crew of 5. it captured the "Z" line, night respectively, A.& B. Coys killed Casualties.4.O.R. EVANS. T. KILLED	
	8/8	1 pm	8/ Cd. JONES. B. and 5.O.R. proceeded to VIEUX BERQUIN along the road having observed a Boche staff moving about 600 yds away. company advanced some of the party to the hut and so twice the Boche did	988.

Army Form C. 2118.

WAR DIARY
or
INTELLIGENCE SUMMARY.

(Erase heading not required.)

2/4 (DENYEO) BATT. R.W.F.

REF.
SHEET. 28.

Vol XXXII Sheet 3.

Place	Date	Hour	Summary of Events and Information	Remarks and references to Appendices
			was then sent to [?]. The patrol having got all their identifications from the body returned to place of exit. No officer & 2 O.R. proceeded to E.17 d 92 where he discovered unoccupied M.G. posts but had sight of recent occupation by night. No enemy were to be seen. In the night of 8-9 C and D/Squadrons our line 250-350 yds. Patrol of 1 N.C.O. and 3 O.R. proceeded to E.11 b 51. E.18 a 23. E.18 b 5. but no enemy there to be seen. Two patrols left our lines at 2 p.m. and proceeded on errands, to E.18 a 00, but before long N°2 got fired on from post at E.18 a 00. N°2 tried to flank it but was fired on from another post at E.18 a 07. the patrol withdrew and with the aid of N°1 patrol tried to ascertain but were machine gunned and bombed. Strength of each post 5 Rank. Two patrols one included an officer and the other an N.C.O. of our lines at 2 p.m. Both patrols were machine gunned. A distance of 50-100 yds were fired on when nearing post on officers & other ranks N°2 patrol observed a party of 10 Rank at E.18 b 34.55. but to get nearer they Rank body withdrew.	
	9	10.40 P.M.	1 N.C.O. & 3 O.R. proceeded to E.18 b 34.55. but were fired on at E.18 a 57 from E.11 G a 07. but were unable to reach the body. A patrol of 1 N.C.O. & 3 O.R. were sent to locate post at E.18 a 42. and to see if it was still occupied. The post was unoccupied. Patrol then proceeded	328.

WAR DIARY or INTELLIGENCE SUMMARY

24 (DEN YEO) BAT. R.W.F.

Vol. XXXII Sheet 4

REF. SHEET 28.

Army Form C. 2118.

Place	Date	Hour	Summary of Events and Information	Remarks and references to Appendices
	10	11pm	T.E 18 a 64 enemy were fired on by outposts named T.E. Post. Fayoho fired 4 rifle grenades before withdrawing. Casualties. 2.O.R. Patrol of 1 N.C.O. 9 + O.R. proceeded to VIEUX BERQUIN along road. They had got some way when they were fired on by a sniper in road. The I.C. being covered by enemy M.G. 1 N.C.O. and 2 O.R. proceeded to E 18 a 87. Patrol 20 strong with 2 M.G. Our patrol fires 6 rifle grenades into the patrol. Silence to our left until 12.50pm. Casualties. 1.O.R.	788.
	11	11.30 pm	Patrol 1 N.C.O. 5 O.R. proceeded to E 17 B 73 ent were held up by enemy at E 17 B 40.25. The patrol tried to work round the wire but were unable to on account of M.G. fire. 2 Lt FERRIS F.G. and 2 6.O.R proceeded with patrol to E 17 a 55.10 – 10.25 –45–15 and found several unoccupied M.G. posts. Some of which was signs of occupation by night. The patrol was fired on by enemy at E 17 B 63.05.	788.
	12	MG	On the night of 11-12 the Battalion was relieved by the 12 R.S.F. The O.Macher losing next took over from 12 NORFOLKS. at K24 C 2510. Sheet 27 S.W. O.R. companies the malaria company parades.	788.

WAR DIARY
or
INTELLIGENCE SUMMARY.

Army Form C. 2118.

2/4 (DEN/VED) BAT. R.W.F.

Instructions regarding War Diaries and Intelligence Summaries are contained in F.S. Regs., Part II. and the Staff Manual respectively. Title pages will be prepared in manuscript.

Vol XXXII Sheet 5

REF. SHEET. 27 & 28

Place	Date	Hour	Summary of Events and Information	Remarks and references to Appendices
	13	9.25 pm	Company parades	#58
	14	9.40pm	Company parades. A draft of 17 O.R. arrived.	#58
	15	9.10pm	Company parades.	#58
	16	10.30 pm	Inspection.	#58
	17	10.15 pm	Company parades	#58
	18	10.25 pm	Inspection of the Battalion by the C.O. General Parade. The Adjutant read out the orders of the Battalion.	#58
	19	pm	Company arrangements. A & B Coy in front, left & right respectively. C & D Coys in "Z" Line Rear. Battn. H.Q. at E.10.c.25.60. Advance E.17.b.6.1.	#58
	20	11.45 pm	The Battalion advanced through the enemy barrage patrols and pushed forward about 500 yds taking over the whole sector from the NORFOLKS.	#58
	21	11 pm	Casualties 1 O.R. NYD GAS. 2 O.R. Patrols pushed forward in the afternoon and succeeded in establishing a line between HULLEBERT Fm F.19.6.9 and BLEU F.19.6.9. The companies then went forward and consolidated.	#58
	22	11.45 pm	Casualties 2 O.R. Sige PHOENIX, J. Keers (NYD Gas. 1 O.R.) Draft 21.O.Rs Patrols pushed forward and 1st Brigade to occupy CUTLET CORNER to BECKET CORNER our left Brigade could not find the left of our	#58

WAR DIARY or INTELLIGENCE SUMMARY

Army Form C. 2118.

24(DEN.YEO) BAT. R.W.F.

REF SHEET. 27.

Vol XXXII Sheet 6

Place	Date	Hour	Summary of Events and Information	Remarks and references to Appendices
			not being able to attain the objective. The Battalion was relieved during the night by the 13th EAST. LANCS.	
			40 DIVISION	
			Casualties 4. OR. KIRK, R. Signs	
	25th	11pm	2/Lt. G.R. ROBERTS. Taken on the strength of the Battalion. The Battalion went to TROCODERO E.9. d.6.8. arriving at 4 a.m.	p.68.
	24th	2/140 pm	The Battalion relieved the 7th Benfords (W.12.a.8.8) Casualties 1.OR. 7 SS. Do C. Coys in the front line X.17.a.43 to X.16.d.1/2. Bat.In H.Q. X.3.d.3505 Casualties (.12OR. NYD. Gas.)	7 SS.
	26th	12pm	Patrols of 1. N.C.O. and 3. O.R. was in conjunction with No 2 Patrol of 1.N.C.O. and 3 O.R.s. proceeded to X.17.C.22. But found no Mg. the enemy Coast Patrols under then proceed to withdraw owing to our artillery fire.	
			Casualties. 3. OR. CASEY, T. Signs.	p 68.
	26th	11.30 pm	Our artillery very active all day. Operations: 2/Lt. D.R. MILES, M.C. Cpl (A/Sergt) McGAIR. D.C.M.	7 SS.
	27th		2 Patrols each of 1.N.C.O. 9 3.OR. proceeded to X.17.c.68.25 to obtain identifications. No MG was found at the Cross Roads, but the MG are believed to have been moved to X.17.c.55 & X.17.c.51.	p.68.

Army Form C. 2118.

WAR DIARY
or
INTELLIGENCE SUMMARY.
(Erase heading not required.)

2/1 (DEN. YEO) BAT, RWF.

REF. SHEET. 27.

Vol XXXI Sheet - 7

Place	Date	Hour	Summary of Events and Information	Remarks and references to Appendices
	27th	10 pm	Our support lines were heavily shelled between 3–7 pm. Casualties I.O.R. C. Jones. 15. West. Yorks. Regt.	p38.
	28th	11.15 pm	Relieved by the Reserve near HONDEGHEM. V.9 & A.7. Arriving there at 4 a.m.	p38.
	29th	10 pm	Company parades.	
	30th	10.15 pm	The Battalion got orders to move to FLETRE leaving HONDEGHEM at 6·30 pm. The Battalion camped round X.10.11.	p38.
	31st	9.30	The Battalion repaired the road through BAILLEUL working from 1·30 – 6 pm.	p38.

J.H. Ley
Lieut Colonel
Comdg 24(DY) Batt RWF.

CONFIDENTIAL.

24 RWF Y86

17 I 8 div
9 C / 31

War Diary.

24th (Denbigh Yeo.) Battalion

Royal Welsh Fusiliers.

Vol. ~~XXXIII~~ IV

Period:—
Sept 1st 1918.
to
Sept 30th 1918.

Army Form C. 2118.

WAR DIARY
or
INTELLIGENCE SUMMARY.

(Erase heading not required.)

24(DEN.YEO) BAT. R.W.F.

REF. SHEET. 27.

Vol XXXIII Sheet 1

Place	Date	Hour	Summary of Events and Information	Remarks and references to Appendices
FLETRE	28/3/18	10 pm	Church Parade in the morning.	
	1/3	9.15 pm	The Battalion received orders to proceed to BAILLEUL but on route reached METEREN counter orders were received to return to FLETRE.	
	3/4	9.30 pm	Company arrangements	
BAILLEUL	4/4	10 pm	The Battalion moved to BAILLEUL S.B.C. and T28a. G.H.Q. Rind. T22c and T28a. Companies proceeded direct from their billets the Transport lines were delayed.	
RIDGE WOOD T18.C	5/4	11 pm	The Battalion relieved the 1st Leinsters @ on HILL 63.B&A Coys. Taking up a position in the front line from T12a82 to T12d50 T18-98, U13a69, U13d15, U13a95, U18d52, U19d-47, C&D Companies in support T18b & ad U18c. Battn H.Q. T18.C 25.80 Battalion Intelligent Report.	
	6/4	11.15 pm	Casualties, 5 O.R. of Battalion wounded. FRANCE. F.G. PTE death. The Battalion held the line for a distance of 1500 yards on a frontage of 1800 yards, undergoing very heavy casualties. The enemy made an attack to the left Company, which was decided by Capt. F.W. MAYHEW. The left of our Company advanced & took up a new position on the French front. Our Company previously U18d. 25.68. All the objectives being taken. U7d.60.95 (U7.d85.95) U7d78.50, U7d38.15. 30 prisoners, 1 L.T.M. and 9 M.G. 85 of the enemy were killed. The Battalion captured	
	7/4	5.30 am	At 5.30 am. The Enemy made another attempt to attack our line but were driven back after a heavy bombardment was put down. Germany dropped on our lines by our Mills grenades, a heavy grenade affective out our lives being lost during the morning.	

WAR DIARY or INTELLIGENCE SUMMARY

24 (DEN YEO) Batt¹¹ R.W.F.
Army Form C. 2118.
REF. MAP. 28. S.W.

Vol. XXIII Sheet 2.

Place	Date	Hour	Summary of Events and Information	Remarks and references to Appendices
	7th		Enemy artillery was exceptionally active all day on our own area. Combatted. Lt J.T. Robinson, (Maunders, S. Jones W. Pte) Killed. 33. Wounded.	SEE
	8th	11 pm	Enemy artillery sustained its activity during the day. None wounded of such extent. On the night of the 8-9th instant The Battalion was relieved by the 1st Royal Irish Rifles and moved into Bde. Support. T28 and T22 a.c. Tks. B.H.q. "C" Coy close Supp[ort] Cobourg Ottes. Pte T.M. Webber Killed. 9. ORS. wounded.	SEE SEE
	9th	1045	Enemy shelled our own area with 5·9 at 10·30 pm	SEE
	10th	10 pm	Enemy again shelled our own area near R.59 about 4·2.	SEE
	11th	11·15 pm	B. Company relieved by "C. Coy".	
	12th	1145 pm	More shelling in the evening by 5·9. A. wounded. Late at night fell on our own area during early hours of the morning. The Battalion was relieved by the 15th West Yorks and marched into Brigade reserve at S.9.d. at 11·30 pm	SEE
S.9.d	13th	8·30 pm	Company arrangements	SEE Rcd
"	14th	10 pm	Nil	off
"	15th	7 pm	Church Parade.	old
S21c	16th	6 pm	Batalion moved from S.9.a. to S.21.c. (Early Strength)	off
"	17th	8 pm	Arranging in Batalion area & Transport Lines	old

WAR DIARY or INTELLIGENCE SUMMARY

Army Form C. 2118.

24th (Bn) (Yeo) Bn. R. Welsh Fus.

Ref map 36 N.W. & 28 S.W.

Vol. XXIII Sheet 3.

Place	Date	Hour	Summary of Events and Information	Remarks and references to Appendices
T.28.a	18th	11 p.m.	The Battalion relieved the 15th Bn West Yorks Regt in the Left Sub-sector of the Left Brigade Sector. Line runs from HYDE PARK CORNER (U.19.d) along MESSINES - PLOEGSTEERT Road, East and S.W. of PLOEGSTEERT. Batt'n H.Q. T.28.a. The 15th West Yorks Rel. made a successful advance of approx J.W. of PLOEGSTEERT in 2 movements. Support Company reconnoitering patrols found much uncertainty during the day. Enemy machine gun & rifle fire active during the relief which started about 6 p.m.	nil
do.	19th	10 p.m.	Patrol 1 N.C.O. & 6 men from U.19.c.9.4 (North of PLOEGSTEERT) to reconnoitre enemy line on U.19.d. No enemy seen. Patrol 1 N.C.O. & 4 men from C.1.a (South of PLOEGSTEERT) to reconnoitre farm house C.1.c.6.6 and compound farm C.1.a.6.1. Inmates found to be strongly held.	nil
T.28.a PETIT POURQUES	20th	11 p.m.	Our H.Q. line relieved with great difficulty owing to heavy shelling of approaches and nature of ground. 3.9" shells in Batt'n H.Q. and vicinity. Shelled down Kemmel by an enemy Battery, N.E. side of DANCOURT & extended down as far as PETIT MONGRE FARM T.33.a.88. Position evacuated + H.Q. installed at U.25.a. to locate enemy guns. Pate R.M LLEWELYN & 6.O.R. proceeded to U.25.a during the day. Guns N.E. from the wood behind Warrington Farm in direction of C.1.c.87, but our observation was not able to locate enemy Batteries + the fact that observation was not hit, small, raiding parties were in want of formed.	nil
do.	21st	11.30 p.m.	Our artillery shelled hostile posts + roads. Enemy artillery intermittently active.	nil

Army Form C. 2118.

WAR DIARY
or
INTELLIGENCE SUMMARY.
(Erase heading not required.)

1/24 (London) B. R. Wh: Fr: Ref. map
                                36 N.W. 28 S.W.
Vol. XXIII Sheet 4

Place	Date	Hour	Summary of Events and Information	Remarks and references to Appendices
T.2.3.d.	21st	Noon	Orders received to proceed to C.1.C.81 (from) of a 40 hours artillery shoot. Embarked on 10 minutes later and proceeded backed by A.4.4 Coy and also some forces of Riflemen. 2/Lt HASON + 7 O.R. received at U.19.a. Fired a No 4 rifle grenades. Ground very difficult in account of natural obstacles. Coy billeted in High Street H.Q.	Killed
	22nd	12 p.m	Orders received to make a diversion to 45 CHEEK Sq. & forwards and attack retreat. Right. Enemy artillery active & machine-gun. Heavy. 2/Lt. R.M. HUGHES & 180.R. proceeded to U.19.d., U.25.b., U.26.a. to attack enemy post. Heard firing on our right + ordered to turn. U.25 being taken by heavy barrage of rifle + m.g. fire + forced to retire. 2 O.R. wounded. 20.R. missing. 1 stretcher Killed. Lt. H.C. KNIGHT and 180.R. proceeded to C.I.C.89, C.I.C.65 to obtain identification. This party was located but unable to reach any enemy. Moonlight, no patrols were able to reach any enemy post. Subsequently given orders by machine gun - Casualties 1 O.R. Killed. 10.R. wounded.	
	23rd	11 p.m.	The 2/14 (London Regt) having slightly advanced the right of their line N. of HYDE PARK CORNER, our Left Coy sent forward to reconnoitre	Rec'd

Army Form C. 2118.

2/4 Budigh Yorks R Welsh Fus.

WAR DIARY
or
INTELLIGENCE SUMMARY.

(Erase heading not required.)

Ref Maps. 36. N.W. 28 S.W. 27.

Volume XXIII Sheet 5.

Instructions regarding War Diaries and Intelligence Summaries are contained in F.S. Regs., Part II. and the Staff Manual respectively. Title pages will be prepared in manuscript.

Place	Date	Hour	Summary of Events and Information	Remarks and references to Appendices
T. 23.d.	24th	11 p.m.	Position for new division front. Enemy artillery very active. Both artilleries active. The Battn was relieved by the 15th Bn W. Yorks Regt. and marched back to BAILLEUL Station.	ditto
HONDEGHEM	25th	9 p.m.	Battn entrained at 3 a.m. at BAILLEUL, and detrained at HAZEBROUCK at 5 a.m. proceeding to HONDEGHEM for 12 days rest, which is badly needed. The men being very tired. Battn. cleaning up kit.	ditto
do.	26th	7 p.m.	ditto	ditto
do.	27th	9 p.m.	Received orders to move up to BAILLEUL as the Brigade is to be in Divisional Reserve in a proposed operation towards WARNETON.	ditto
T 25 c.11. (Sh.28)	28th	11.30 p.m.	Battn left HONDEGHEM and entrained at HAZEBROUCK at 11.30 a.m. detraining at BAILLEUL at 12.15 p.m. The Battalion was carried at full railway speed to point no. Marched to company at X 24 a 3.4. (W.H BAILLEUL at 10 p.m. The Battn marched to T 25 c 11.	ditto
U.14. a. Central	29th	11 p.m.	The Battalion remained in the Company until 3 a.m. when it moved forward to U.14.a Central (The BAKERY) on the PLOEGSTEERT—MESSINES ROAD. No casualties were sustained on its march. The enemy artillery active on HICE 63, firing H.E. + Gas shells. The intensive operations in the north sector resulted (considerable gmt.) in the capture of ground S.E. 001 of GAPAARD by the 93rd Brig. Bde. and the line was advanced in PLOEGSTEERT WOOD to the 92nd S.B. By nightfall	ditto
U.14. a.central.30		10.30 p.m.	the position in PLOEGSTEERT WOOD remained cleared up, and in the morning of the 30th, the advance was continued. The 12 Norfolk Regt worked down the	

D.D. & L., London, E.C.
(A10560) Wt W. 1304/P713 750,000 4/18 Sch. 52 Forms/C2118/16

24' (Sealign Yeo) Bn R. Welsh Fus-

WAR DIARY
or
INTELLIGENCE SUMMARY
(Erase heading not required.)

Army Form C. 2118.

Ref maps
36 N.W. 28 S.W. 27.

Vol XXIII Sheet 6.

Place	Date	Hour	Summary of Events and Information	Remarks and references to Appendices
(contd)	30.		East edge of the WOOD. B.Coy 24 RWF (which had moved forward the previous night to U.15.b.) came under the command of O.C. 12/ Norfolks for the operation but remained in position in U.15.b. throughout the day. At 7.30 p.m. the Battalion moved back to camp at X 24 a 3.4. (ANCH of BAILLEUL) WARNETON - the line of the WARNAVE BECQUE - RIVER LYS having been obtained. Heavy shelling by the enemy on our support system in U. 14.a central on 29th. Both H.E. & gas shells. Casualties. Lieut (A/Capt) A.T. THOMAS (Glamorgan Yeo. attd). Sgt Stonnar & Pte Evans killed. 5 O.R. wounded. The weather during 29 & 30 was very wet, and the Battn had no cover.	
			Officer Reinforcements:-	
			23/9/18. 2nd Lt R. COURT from 3rd RWF	
			" T. BROADHURST Do	
			" F.E. KIPPEN Do	
			" J.H.C. CAMPBELL Do	
			25/9/18 2nd Lt J.M.R. THOMAS Do	
			E.H. BENNETT Do	

[signatures]
Comdg 24 (D) Batt. R.W.F.

CONFIDENTIAL

94(Yeo)/31

18 I

WAR DIARY

24ᵀᴴ (DENBIGH YEO.) BN. R. WELSH FUSILIERS

OCTOBER 1918

VOLUME ~~XXXIV~~
V

PERIOD:- OCTOBER 1ˢᵀ 1918
TO
OCTOBER 31ˢᵀ 1918.

24th (Denbigh Yeo.) Bn.
Royal Welch Fusiliers

WAR DIARY or **INTELLIGENCE SUMMARY**
(Erase heading not required.)

Army Form C. 2118.

Ref Maps Sheet 28.

Instructions regarding War Diaries and Intelligence Summaries are contained in F. S. Regs., Part II. and the Staff Manual respectively. Title pages will be prepared in manuscript. VOL XXXIV Sheet 1.

Place	Date	Hour	Summary of Events and Information	Remarks and references to Appendices
X 24 & 34	1	8/am	Baths, Cleaning up, etc.	E.M.
do	2	7/am	Training	E.M.
do	3	6/pm	Inspections & Training	E.M.
do	4	7/pm	-do-	E.M.
do	5	8/am	Training	E.M.
T18.C.31.	6	11.30pm	Relieved 13th Works Lancs. Regt. in Brigade Reserve in the region of PETIT MUNCQUE FARM and HYDE PARK CORNER	E.M.
do	7	11.00pm	Training & Salvage Work	E.M.
do	8	11.40pm	-do-	E.M.
U.16 & 5	9	11.10pm	Relieved 12th Roy. Scots Fusrs. in Left Battalion Sector (C.2.) Three Companies in front line extending from a point 1000 yds. No. of PONT-ROUGE and following the line of the River LYS through WARNETON to BAS-WARNETON.	E.M.
do	10	10pm	Quiet during day. Save for intermittent enemy shelling along our front. Vigorous patrolling throughout the night to reconnoitre the West Bank of the LYS and report on bridges or crossing places if any. A patrol crossed the river at one point by means of a sunken	E.M.
	11		Pont (Bridge) were subjected to enemy M.G. and T.M. fire.	

WAR DIARY
or
INTELLIGENCE SUMMARY.
(Erase heading not required.)

Army Form C. 2118.

Place	Date	Hour	Summary of Events and Information	Remarks and references to Appendices
U16.d-8.5		11.10 p.m.	Two feint attacks on enemy position in the form of Artillery creeping barrage. First barrage fell on enemy front line trench E. of the LYS and continued for 30 minutes covering the area from FME. DURIEZ to BROKEN CHIMNEY, our heavy artillery at the same time bombarding FRELINGHIEN, and our M.G. L.G. and rifles cooperating. The second and similar barrage fell at 1015 on the area E. of the LYS, extending from a point 500 yds N.N.W. of DEULEMENT to the SPINNING MILL on the road between DEULEMENT and WARNETON-SUD. This lasted for 30 minutes, the heavies at the same time bombarding DEULEMENT and Seng. Counter Battery work. Careful observation was kept of any enemy action during these feint attacks, and location of his M.G. and T. Ms ascertained also the length of time taken for him to put down his barrage, and the time of same. Slight enemy shelling during the day. Enemy O.Ps. were engaged by our Artillery	E.M.

WAR DIARY
or
INTELLIGENCE SUMMARY.
(Erase heading not required.)

Army Form C. 2118.

Place	Date	Hour	Summary of Events and Information	Remarks and references to Appendices
U.16.b.8.5	12	11 p.m.	Enemy started a barrage along the LYS and across our front, especially along the PONT ROUGE – WARNETON road, at 0530. At 0645 their bombardment slacks 26 minutes, commenced by us on UNCURL TRENCH, FME. DURIEZ, UDDER TRENCH, WARNETON SUD and MARIE. Lots in day enemy observes evacuating wounded. Occasional enemy shelling. Relieved by 18th Bn. East Yorks Regt. Marches back to SWINDON CAMP near BAILLEUL.	E.M. E.M.
U.16.b.6.3	13	6 p.m.	Nil.	E.M.
-do-	14	6 p.m.	Cleaning up.	E.M.
-do-	15	6 p.m.	Training.	E.M.
T.25.c.14.16	16	10 p.m.	Moves to Camp of BAILLEUL – ARMENTIERS Road and near DE BROEKEN ROAD and took over from 18th D.L.I. in the Support area.	E.M.
U.23.b.17.17	17	9 p.m.	Moves forward to positions in vicinity of the junction of PLOEGSTEERT and PONT ROUGE – WARNETON roads	E.M.

WAR DIARY
or
INTELLIGENCE SUMMARY.

(Erase heading not required.)

Army Form C. 2118.

Place	Date	Hour	Summary of Events and Information	Remarks and references to Appendices
J.23.b.17	18	1800	Battalion employed on improving PONT ROUGE – WARNETON ROAD	AM
do	19	1900	Training	AM
G.16.a.75.99	20	2100	Marched to billets in LANNOY	AM
do	21	1800	Inspections & training	AM
do	22	17.00	Company Inspections & Training	AM
do	23	1600	Training	AM
do	24	1900	Company Training. Ranges, Schemes and Classes	AM
G.16.a.77.60 / S.22.a.99	25	1800	Marched to MOUSCRON starting at 0815 to billets in that school	AM
S.22.a.99	26	1700	Marched to STACEGHEM to billets in farms	AM
I.20.Central	27	1900	Marched to DEERLYCK " "	AM
I.20.cen	28	1700	Cleaning up A.C. Rifles EMB & equipment ready for the line	AM
P.7.a.2.8	29	1600	Marched to VEERKE. Relieved 10th E. YORKs night of 29/30. Enemy garrisoning	AM
P.7.a.2.8	30	1900	Enemy line vicinity INGOYCHEN. Fairly heavy S, 9 & 2 Gas Shelling few casualties	AM
P.7.a.2.8	31	1600	Operations Battalion advanced the line to E. of GASTER capturing	AM
P.6 C.2.8	(31)	1700	10 field guns & about 250 prisoners. Time did not permit other material being counted	AM

1/11/18 McAlpin Major
OC ~ 16th RWF

CONFIDENTIAL

19-I
5 sheets

WAR DIARY

24TH (DENBIGH YEO.) BN. ROYAL WELSH FUSILIERS.

NOVEMBER 1918.

VOL. XXXV.

PERIOD:- Nov. 1st 1918
TO
NOV. 30TH. 1918.

Army Form C. 2118.

WAR DIARY
or
INTELLIGENCE SUMMARY.

Vol. XXXV Sheet I
1918

(Erase heading not required.)

Place	Date	Hour	Summary of Events and Information	Remarks and references to Appendices
Sheet 29 DI C 20	Nov. 1st	1900	Operation Battle advanced to Knits & but occupied on Nunte	
			R5 C 24 — R5 d 9.8 SWEVEGEM. Causing one L.E. Nov? 1st to casualties	
P L C 28	2nd	1500	Holding the line between R5 d98 to R6 a56&b1 S²R2 50 d m to K6b sheeting	
"	"	1700	Relief by 24 Bn 33rd Brigade Relief complete 0600 on Nov 3rd	
Sheet 29 N14 d 20	3		Proceeded to LANTEN (J 3 L C 1 d) marched to LAUWE Mattegling 1230	
"	4th	1800	Marched from Cantine to LAUWE Mattegling 1330 Cleaning up & checking stores	
"	5	1900	Cleaning up & Rifle Inspection & Batts	
"	6	1600	Chew Bos LAUWE Rifle Inspection & Chew Brit	
"	7	1900	Inspection of Rifles cleaning Brit but	
"	8	7 pm	Battalion Parade on Stringhouse for Inspection by C.O. Viewing Company bundles 830 Battery Route March 1030 -1230	
"	9	1730	Parades 0815 -1015 Physical Training & Bayonet fighting 1030 -1230 further Route March	
P 29 a 6.2	10	1200	Battalion moved from LAUWE to AVELGHEM via COURTRAI, SWEVEGHEM, arriving 16.15	
N 46 c 35	11	2100	" AVELGHEM to RENAIX via RUGGE TUYEN ORROIR RUSSEIGNIES " 11.30	
"	12	1700	Battalion halted on the German tracks at Barracks Marked by Transport	
V 25 94	13	1500	Battalion moved to ORROIR via RUSSEIGHEM ANVAGIES arrived 1215	

WAR DIARY
or
INTELLIGENCE SUMMARY.
(Erase heading not required.)

Army Form C. 2118.

Vol. VI Sheet 2
1918

Place	Date	Hour	Summary of Events and Information	Remarks and references to Appendices
Sheet 29	Nov			
D.1c.75	14	1645	Battalion moved from ORROIR to SWEVEGHEM via RUYEN RUGGE AVELGHEM arriving 1240	See
M.4c.8.3	15	2000	SWEVEGHEM to LAUWE via COURTRAI MARCKE 1445	See
"	16	15.00	General cleaning up Parade. 2 New Officers arrived 2nd Lt Hughes, 3rd Lt Crawshaw. Present at which Lt.Col. O.C. Division was	Ens.
"	17	0900	Church Parade of Thanksgiving. Brigade Service at which G.O.C. Division was	Ens.
"	18	0900	Brigade Parade and Bn Drill. Afternoon – Football and Sports	Ens.
"	19	"	Bn. Parade & Coy. Training. Afternoon 1st Football Competition	Ens.
"	20	"	" " Football Completion & marching past.	Ens.
"	21	0900	Brigade Parade and marching past. Afternoon Football	Ens.
"	22	1030	94th Brigade was inspected by the G.O.C. 31st Division who presented ribands to medal winners & was very pleased with the general turnout	Ens.
"	23	0900	Batta. By the order of the Brigadier the day was kept as a holiday in recognition of the excellence of the Parade of yesterday. Col. McLagn Lr. Colling joined 12th Bn	Ens.
"	24	0830	Bn. left LAUWE to German Hutments at Sheet 28 Q.5.d.4.2 Arrival 12.30 via Menin	Ens.
Sheet 28				
Q.5.d.4.2	25	0815	Bn. moved to Poperinge along the Menin Road to YPRES thence by the main road to POPERINGHE Arrival at H.1690	Ens.

WAR DIARY or INTELLIGENCE SUMMARY.

Army Form C. 2118.

Vol. VI Sheet 3 1918.

(Erase heading not required.)

Place	Date	Hour	Summary of Events and Information	Remarks and references to Appendices
Selsoeges HAZEBROUCK 2 I.	Nov 26	0900	Left Poperinghe for old Bombing School at Iydyghem. March via ABEELE & STEENVOORDE ARR. at TERDEGHEM 1300. (REF. HAZEBROUCK 1/100,000 3G)	Ens
3G	27	1000	Bn moved from TERDEGHEM to RENESCURE via CASSEL – BAVINCHOVE & LE NIEPPE Arr. at RENESCURE at 1500	Ens
4E	28	1000	Left RENESCURE for TATINGHEM via ARQUES & LONGUENESSE Arrived at 1500 at Jalinghem	Ens
4C	29	0900	Cleaning up & rifle inspection.	
4C	30	0900	Bn kit inspection by C.O. 143.O.R. joined the Bn from France.	Ens

A.C. Leyhill Lt-Col
14/18 Cincy Inf. R.W.F.

CONFIDETIAL.

WAR DIARY.

24th (Denbigh Yeo) Bn. Royal Welsh Fusiliers.

December 1918

Volume ~~XXXVI~~ VII

On His Majesty's Service

Period :- December 1st 1918
To
December 31st 1918.

CONFIDETIAL.

Army Form C. 2118.

WAR DIARY
or
INTELLIGENCE SUMMARY, Vol. 36

24th (DENBIGH YEO) BATTn RWF

Sheet 1. Dec 1918.

(Erase heading not required.)

Place	Date	Hour	Summary of Events and Information	Remarks and references to Appendices
ST OMER COMBINED SHEET X7 Central	Dec. 1st	10.00	Sunday Services Nil.	
"	2	"	Owing to overcrowding of billets at Yatinghem "B" Coy move to village of Cormette (Q 34 central) Col. Clegg takes command of the Bn on return from Hospital	
"	3	9.00	Coy Parades and inspection. Afternoon Nil.	
"	4	9.00	Coy Parade Nil.	
"	5	"	"	
"	6	8.45	Bn. Parade to march to WISQUES (2ND ARMY SCHOOL) to witness a demonstration by the Demonstration Platoon of Drill, Recreational Training	
"	7	9.00	Coy. Parades Nil	
"	8	10.00	Sunday Services Nil	
"	9	9.00	Coy Parades. One Coy. Salvage work	
"	10	9.00	Salvage work and filling in trenches on the TATINGHEM—ETREHEM Road	
"	11	9.00	Bn moves from YATINGHEM and district and proceed to the camp of the 2ND ARMY MUSKETRY CAMP at LUMBRES (SHEET 36 D.S.d.) ELEVEN Mins moved for Demobilation	

Army Form C. 2118.

WAR DIARY
or
INTELLIGENCE SUMMARY.
(Erase heading not required.)

Vol. 30 Sheet 2. Dec. 1918

Instructions regarding War Diaries and Intelligence Summaries are contained in F.S. Regs., Part II. and the Staff Manual respectively. Title pages will be prepared in manuscript.

Place	Date	Hour	Summary of Events and Information	Remarks and references to Appendices
SHEET 36 D EAST. 5 d.	12.	800	Twenty five miners proceed to HAZEBROUCK for demobilisation	
	13.	900	Coy Parades and Education	
	14.	"	" "	nil
	15.	1000	Ten miners proceed for Demobilisation. Sunday Service. Nine miners proceed.	
	16.	900	Coy Parades.	
	17.	800	Eleven miners sent away. Bn. moves to new Hutments N. of Lumbres at W.25c.4.8	
ST. OMER COMBINED SHEET W25c.4.8	18	900	Nil.	
	19		Improvement of Camp.	
	20		nil.	
	21.		Parades and inspection	
	22.		Sunday Parade Services	
	23		nil	
	24		Xmas Eve.	

Army Form C. 2118.

WAR DIARY
or
INTELLIGENCE SUMMARY.

(Erase heading not required.)

Vol. 7 Sheet 3

Instructions regarding War Diaries and Intelligence Summaries are contained in F. S. Regs., Part II. and the Staff Manual respectively. Title pages will be prepared in manuscript.

Place	Date	Hour	Summary of Events and Information	Remarks and references to Appendices
St Omer COMBINED SHEET W.25.C.4 &	25	1000	Christmas Day Service	
	26.	900	Bn. Parade. Nil.	
	27.	800	20 men proceed for Demobilisation	
	28.		nil	
"	29.	900	One Coy. Salvage work at WISQUES Coy Parades	
"	30.		Salvage work	
"	31.		nil.	

J. H. Clegg
Lieut-Colonel.
24 (Derby) Batt'n Reg't.

CONFIDENTIAL

War Diary

24th (Denbigh Yeo.) Bn. Royal Welch Fusiliers.

Jan. 1919.

Vol VIII ~~XXXVII~~

Period. Jan 1st. 1919
To.
Jan 31st. 1919

Sheet I.

2/4 "(Denbigh Yeo) Battⁿ R.W.F.

Army Form C. 2118.

WAR DIARY
or
INTELLIGENCE SUMMARY.
(Erase heading not required.)

VOL. 8 SHEET 1. JAN. 1919

Place	Date	Hour	Summary of Events and Information	Remarks and references to Appendices
ST OMER COMBINED SHEET W 25.6.4.8	JAN. 1	-	Nil. 2 Long Service men demobilised. Ration strength of Bn. 673	
	2.	-	5 men demobilised	M.2.
	3.	-	2 " "	
	4.	-	1 man "	
	5.	-	2/Lt. Broadhurst M.C. proceeds for Demobilization.	
	6	-	nil.	
	7	-	nil	
	8	-	nil.	
	9	-	nil	
	10	-	nil	
	11	-	nil	
	12	-	2/Lt CAMPBELL & 20 men (mostly Miners) proceed Home for Demobilization	
	13	-	2/Lt SUTTON & 62 ORs (mostly Farmers) proceed for Demobilization	

SHEET 2

Army Form C. 2118.

2/4 (Ralph Yeo) Batt'n R.W.F.

WAR DIARY
or
INTELLIGENCE SUMMARY.
(Erase heading not required.)

Vol. 8. Sheet 2. Jan 1919

Instructions regarding War Diaries and Intelligence Summaries are contained in F. S. Regs., Part II. and the Staff Manual respectively. Title pages will be prepared in manuscript.

Place	Date	Hour	Summary of Events and Information	Remarks and references to Appendices
ST OMER COMBINED SHEET W 25. C. 4. 8	JAN 13.		The Brigadier presents Medal ribbands to Officers and men who have recently been awarded decorations. Bn. loses 1st & only Dvr Cpl to R.S.F.	
	14, 15, 16, 17		Nil.	
	18		Lt. BAILEY + 5 O.R. demobilised	
	19		10 O.R. leave the Bn.	
	20		Lt LLEWELLYN & 100 R leave for Demobilisation	Ends
	21		5 men demobilised	
	22		2/Lt ROWSE & 6 O.R. demobilised	
	23 & 24		Nil	
	25		Capt. A. W. MAYHEW & 36 O.R. demobilised	
	26		2/Lt EASTWOOD & 17 O.R. leave for Demob.	
	27		Capt Hodges, 2/Lt Hughes " " "	
	28		19 O.R leave the Bn.	
	29		12 O.R leave the Bn. The Battalion move from LUMBRES to HONDEGHEM via HAZEBROUCK in Motor Lorries & settle down at the Staging Camp.	
	30.		The Bn. relieves the 26th R.W.F. of the Staging Camp duties	
	31		Nil. Ration strength of Bn. 398 as compared with 673 on 12th Jan.	

CONFIDENTIAL

WAR DIARY

24th (Denbigh Yeo.) Bn. R. Welsh Fusiliers

FEBUARY 1919.

VOLUME 38

Period February 1st 1919.
To
February 28th 1919.

Army Form C. 2118.

WAR DIARY
or
INTELLIGENCE SUMMARY.
(Erase heading not required.)

Vol. 38 Sheet 1. Feb. 1919.

Place	Date	Hour	Summary of Events and Information	Remarks and references to Appendices
HONDEGHEM STAGING CAMP	Feb. 1.	—	Camp Duties. 25 men moved to HAZEBROUCK for demobilisation	
	2.	—	ditto 43 " " " " " "	
	3.	—	" 45 " " " " " "	End
	4.	—	nil	
	5.	—	1,500 troops have though the camp	
	6.		Camp duties More troops pass through	
	8.		" "	
	9.		nil	
	10.		nil	
	11.		nil	
	12.		nil	
	13.		Lt. KNIGHT & 4 men demobilised	
	14.		Seven men demobilised	
	15.		Two " " "	
	16.		One " " "	
	17.		nil —	
	18.		nil —	End

Instructions regarding War Diaries and Intelligence Summaries are contained in F.S. Regs., Part II. and the Staff Manual respectively. Title pages will be prepared in manuscript.

Army Form C. 2118.

WAR DIARY
or
INTELLIGENCE SUMMARY.
(Erase heading not required.)

Instructions regarding War Diaries and Intelligence Summaries are contained in F. S. Regs., Part II. and the Staff Manual respectively. Title pages will be prepared in manuscript.

Place	Date	Hour	Summary of Events and Information	Remarks and references to Appendices
HONDIGHEM.	Feb./9.		Presentation of Colours by Gen. Butler. Owing to demobilization proceeding so rapidly only 12 Off. and 116 O.Rs. on parade. Lt. Hough in charge of Colour party.	
	" 20.		7 O.Rs. demobilized.	
	" 21.		100 O.Rs. demobilized. Col. Clegg takes over command of the Brigade.	N.H.
	" 22.		" "	
	" 23.		" "	
	" 24.		Looking to report.	
	" 25.		Strength down to 182.	
	" 26.		1 agent of indisc.	
	" 27.		2 O.Rs. demobilized.	
	" 28.		7 O.Rs. demobilized.	

CONFIDENTIAL

1915

23 I
4 sheets

WAR DIARY

24ᵀᴴ (DENBIGH YEO.) BN. R. WELSH FUSILIERS.

MARCH 1919.

VOLUME XXXIX

PERIOD:- MARCH 1ˢᵀ 1919.
TO.
MARCH 31ˢᵀ 1919.

Army Form C. 2118.

Vol 39. Sheet 1. March 1919

WAR DIARY
or
INTELLIGENCE SUMMARY.
(Erase heading not required.)

Instructions regarding War Diaries and Intelligence Summaries are contained in F. S. Regs., Part II. and the Staff Manual respectively. Title pages will be prepared in manuscript.

Place	Date	Hour	Summary of Events and Information	Remarks and references to Appendices
HONDIGHEM.	March 1st		Nothing of interest.	
	2nd		Sunday. No services held.	
	3rd		2 ORs. Demobilized. The Cadre demobilized	
	4th		the Batt - move in lorries to St Omer and take up sleeping quarters in the P.O.W. Camp near the Canal. The weather has taken a turn for the worse and rained nearly all day.	
	5th		Still raining.	
	6th		Nothing to report. The rain keeps up & the weather bad.	
	7th		Nothing to report. The weather still very bad.	
	8th		Much better (sun shining)	
	9th		2 ORs demobilized	
	10th		Nothing to report. Capt. Cole goes to Hospital.	
	11th		Weather much better.	
	12th		Nothing to report.	
	13th		2nd Lt Chowen Returns from U.K.	
	14th		Nothing to report	
St. Omer.	15th		Detachment at Houdeghem returns in lorries to Unit	
	16th		The volunteers & deturnables for the Army of occupation proceeded to form the 6th S.W.B.s at Dunkirk by rail entraining St Omer 06-00.	

Army Form C. 2118.

WAR DIARY
or
INTELLIGENCE SUMMARY.
(Erase heading not required.)

Vol 39. Sheet 2. March 1919

Instructions regarding War Diaries and Intelligence Summaries are contained in F. S. Regs., Part II. and the Staff Manual respectively. Title pages will be prepared in manuscript.

Place	Date	Hour	Summary of Events and Information	Remarks and references to Appendices
St. Omer	March 17th		Nothing to report	
	18th		Nothing to report	
	19th		Nothing to report	
	20th		Morris detachment returned to Unit.	
	21st		Nothing to report.	
	22nd		Nothing to report	
	23rd		A football match (soccer) took place between the 94th & Brigade and a team of the French. The latter being far superior & thoroughly deserved their win by 5 goals to 2.	
	24th		Nothing to report.	
	25th		2nd Lieut. C.A. Miller left for demobilization	
	26th		Nothing to report	
	27th		Nothing to report.	
	28th		2nd Lieuts. C.A. Clarke & J.J. Crawshaw left for Demob.	
	29th		Snow falling heavily	
	30th		2nd Lieut. Mahon leaves for duty at Merris.	
	31st		2nd Lieut. E.W. Savours leaves for Demobilization	

Willis Major Commanding 94th (10.) Bn R.W.F.

Army Form C. 2118.

WAR DIARY
or
INTELLIGENCE SUMMARY.
(Erase heading not required.)

Instructions regarding War Diaries and Intelligence Summaries are contained in F.S. Regs. Part II. and the Staff Manual respectively. Title pages will be prepared in manuscript.

24R WF
Vol 40 Sheet 1. April 1919
WA/6

Place	Date	Hour	Summary of Events and Information	Remarks and references to Appendices
St Omer	April 1st		Nothing of interest.	
	2nd		Nothing to report.	
	3rd		Cleaning of S.S. waggons	
	4th		2 O.Rs returned from leave in UK. These being retained proceeded by rail to join the 6th S.W.B.	
	5th		at PONT DE BRIQUES.	
	6th		Nothing to report	
	7th		Nothing to report	
	8th		Inspection of Kit etc.	
	9th		Nothing to report	
	10th		2nd Lieut 'Mahan leaves for UK as Regular.	
	11th		Nothing to report.	
	12th		2nd Lieut D.H. Hughes returned from leave in UK.	
	13th		Nothing to report.	
			Nothing to report	

Army Form C. 2118.

WAR DIARY
or
INTELLIGENCE SUMMARY.
(Erase heading not required.)

Vol no Sheet 2. April 1919

Place	Date	Hour	Summary of Events and Information	Remarks and references to Appendices
St Omer	April 14		Nothing to report.	
	15th		Nothing to report.	
	16th		Nothing to report.	
	17th		2 O.R's proceeded to join the 6th Bn. O.N.B.	
	18th		Nothing to report.	
	19th		Lt. H. A. Bleakly leaves unit for Demobilisation. Capts A. B. Looney and Lt. W. B. Kimberly leave today for Duty in U.K. as Conducting Officers.	
	20th		2/Lt. W. McBoy Granted Official Leave to UK.	
	21st		Lt. W. O. Jackson returned from Leave.	
	22nd		2/Lt. J Jackson returned from leave.	
	23rd		Nothing to report.	
	24th		Nothing to report.	

Army Form C. 2118.

WAR DIARY
or
INTELLIGENCE SUMMARY.
(Erase heading not required.)

Vol 40 Sheet 3 April 1919

Place	Date	Hour	Summary of Events and Information	Remarks and references to Appendices
St. Omer.	April 25th		Bus trips arranged for 2 days, at Lille, Calais, etc. Party from Bde. left for Lille at 9.30 this morning.	
	26th		Three Officers proceed to P. of War Companies and proceeded today. – 2/Lt W. D. Morrison and 2/Lt A. J. Buckton to 317 Coy Werwicq; 2/Lt J. Jackson M.M. to 313 Coy Calais. Party returned about 17.00 hours today from Lille.	
	27th		Nothing to report.	
	28th		Nothing to report.	
	29th		Nothing to report.	
	30th		Nothing to report.	

Geo Clive Capt. & Adjt.
74th (D.H.V.) Bn. R.E.C.F.

30/4/19

www.ingramcontent.com/pod-product-compliance
Lightning Source LLC
Chambersburg PA
CBHW081453160426
43193CB00013B/2461